JUANITA NENA RUDONBEEKE

BITTER SWEET

Poems of Reflection

JUANITA NENA RUDONBEEKE

BITTER SWEET

Poems of Reflection

MEMOIRS
Cirencester

Published by Memoirs

MEMOIRS
PUBLISHING

25 Market Place, Cirencester, Gloucestershire, GL7 2NX
info@memoirsbooks.co.uk www.memoirspublishing.com

ISBN: 978-1909304154

Printed in England

ACKNOWLEDGEMENTS

It is with the sincerest of thanks that I must acknowledge my husband Trevor and sons Andrew and Kevin for all the wonderful support they have given me throughout this project. Special thanks to my sister Margaret-Rose for constantly being there at the end of the phone listening, commenting and offering advice with no regard as to the time of day. Without them this book would not have been completed.

Thank you.

Juanita Nena RudonBeeke

Poems of Reflection

BITTERSWEET

Poems of Reflection

A CHILD'S FEAR

Night time has come and to bed she will go
Her head she will lay down
Her eyes are open but will not close
She knows what is about to come

Her hands she clasps as in prayer
For a night without fear
For when her eyes are shut
Something evil seems to appear

As it looks down at her
With eyes so striking red
Her eyes now open
Her body now fixed to the bed

She tries to scream, no sound she makes
She tries to stir, no movement comes
And all this time it stares at her
This presence here, an ungodly fear

It is now half five and the church bells ring
She knows now she can rise
The sun is out, the sky is blue
And sounds now she can make

Her hands in prayer she offers thanks
For now she will close her eyes
For tonight she knows she must be prepared
For again it will appear

A BARREN ROAD

The most unfortunate road a woman could walk
Is the road of barrenness
A cruel road of whys and tears
A road of loneliness

She'll have her times of sobbing
When others are expecting
She'll often hold her hands in woe
All this behind closed dwelling

She'll rage at God of how unfair
She cannot have a child
He is the creator of life after all
So why not implant in her?

This love for being a mother
This means beyond compare
She'll tell how others can
And they don't even care

And when that special time arrives
The eventful 'Mother's Day'
She'll watch all beaming mothers
A member of this league she's nay

It's hard to imagine what she's feeling
It's all about understanding
God's gift of children is not where or why
It's about how He gives His blessings

A BROKEN PROMISE

A beautiful red rose – a promise he made
For each year we spent as our love we declared
The roses I kept and each time I prayed
Our love for each other will never be betrayed

The years they passed, no red rose came my way
It was replaced by those grown on the way
And each new year my red rose I think
And dreamed of its petals all scattered in the wind

And now in return my life is upside down
Our love for each other seemed all but gone
No rose or daffodil can mend this broken heart
And a promise made that was taken apart

A CHILD'S CHRISTMAS GIFT

Are we in control or are we of guilt
In the new meaning of Christmas
Where toys of war and violence
Are the joys we bring to our kids?

The sounds in the stores are all of bangs
And *rat-at-tat-tats* of guns
And lipsticks and cream to your four-year-old
And high heels fit for a queen

And then we say – no – not we
And yet we do but buy
No matter the cost and yet we find
And still to our kids we give

I raise my hand and accept this guilt
To my children this I did teach
For this they know and this they'll share
To their own kids I do believe

So parents beware and dispel this thought
Before it becomes too late
Think what you buy for your child this time
Or look forward to a life of guilt

A CHILD'S FACE

A child's face is an image
A picture to behold
There's joy and elation
There's pleasure and emotion

When they look you in the eye
It reaches your very soul
And when they laugh with you
You hug them even more

An innocence is captured
A priceless definition
That can only be patent
On the face of an infant

A CHRISTMAS MESSAGE

One cold and very silent night
I find myself just trembling
At the news of a baby's birth
And the reason He was sent on earth

A tale that's told of this baby's life
And the journey taken on a bitter path
To save us from sin and to die on a cross
As proof of his love for us here on earth

I then think of you people of this world
And your thoughts this Christmas day
This advent season I see you cheer
But what's your meaning – I do but fear

I see allegation – I see rejection
I see hunger and then thirst
I see refusal – I see denial
But taken, there's no action

Houses are covered with twinkling lights
Trees all shimmer with gold
Dancing music and drinks just flow
The intent – but to put on a show

Think back my people I beg of you
Of the true meaning of Christmas
Where peace and love was the game
And the reason our Saviour was born

My heart it aches with sorrow and woe
And the message today we're portraying
Think of the babe and the message sent
Stop his heart from crying

Come you believers, come one and all
Veer from this path we've created
Bend down and pay homage to Our King
As Peace and Love we bring

A DESTITUTE'S CHRISTMAS

All day long and weeks on end
No food to eat – no bed to sleep
No blanket to keep my body warm
This fate of mine it seems must keep

Wasn't born this way but now I'm here
Perhaps a making of my own
Then the thought of how I was neglected
When I used to live at home

I'm outside here in the freezing cold
And my tears they seem so frozen
As I look in the sky at the morning star
My one wish but to join her there

To feel the magic this Christmas night
To forget the needs and woes
To feel the touch of a saintly hand
Upon my fevered brow

I sit here alone and wait my demise
And think of the birth of a little child
Our saviour who was born this night
Our Lord Emmanuel – Jesus Christ

And as this thought it comes to mind
I get the feel of peace
Like me he was a destitute
As He fled to Galilee

A FATHER'S SIN

Four years old and fast in slumber
You'd think she would be safe
Then came along one she knew
And tucked himself beside her

His hands he lay on her little body
But this she does not mind
After all he that's lying there
Is no other than her Dad

What happens next is beyond belief
Of what is about to happen
Her little body is completely smothered
As this man covers her with his own

O please dear God, please let him stop
Why is my good Dad bad?
Why is he hurting me so like this
O God please let him stop

This four-year-old is now disturbed
And really quite confused
The show of fear and crying she makes
Whenever she sees her Dad

She does not eat, she cannot sleep
She always turns away
This matter she just can't speak of
For in her they won't believe

A MEANS TO NO END

Where is he when you are down?
He's always around but not to be found
This person you gave your whole life to
This one you'll defend through right and wrong

The tears you've shed – your body it aches
There's the hurt and the pain, a means to no end
But when the time comes and he is in need
He'll call and expects you to be there

Oh for the strength and oh for the courage
For one day he will call
He'll see for himself – just how he will fare
For you see – I will not be there

A MOTHER'S TEARS

Many a tear is shed
From the eyes of a loving mother
No one seems to know why
And no one ever will

When questions are asked by a child
As to why their mothers cry
The answer is very simple
For nought they say is why

But that is where they're wrong
For mothers are really strong
They are rather special
With shoulders there to cry on

An inner strength when giving birth
To rejection when her child grows up
She carries on when others submits
And tries not to show her hurt

Through illness and in health you'll find
Her care for you is special
To comfort and protect her child
And this without condescension

When tears you see her cry
This is but her only weakness
Her staying power now comes down
To shed for a love so strong

A NOVEMBER SALUTE

Soldiers, Sailors, Wing Men too
All dead men of WWII
Courage and honour you have shown
Around the world for your nation

Soldiers, Sailors, Wing Men too
All brave women that follow you
Support they've given to their fallen men
Around the world for their nation

Soldiers, Sailors, Wing Men too
The sacrifice, strength, and fortitude
We honour you this November morn
As around the world we all shall mourn

Children, teens and adults salute
Bow your heads and pay tribute
To the men and women of WWII
Whose lives were laid down – for you

A PLACE THAT WAS –
A PLACE NOW IS

Strikingly beautiful this coral isle
That sits there in a warm green sea
With skies of blue and sandy beach
An array of colours quite a display

Flora, fauna, and a coral reef
Palm trees sway in a gentle breeze
Tropic climes and blue lagoons
Stars dance as they partner the moon

Sounds can be heard in the early morn
Where rhythm and drums are the norm
As the dawn breaks the people are one
In this beautiful isle that sits in the sun

A place that was – a place now is
She still sits there in her emerald seas
Where its flora, fauna, and coral reef
Are being pilfered for economic greed

A place that was – a place now is
Where the rhythm stays but you can't sway
For now its people that once were one
Now live in fear from daggers and guns

A place that was – but still now is
This beautiful place I once called home
A paradise then – but now is gone
A paradise lost – it has now become

A SENSELESS ACT

O Lord forgive them that's killing us all
As we fathom to know the reason why
But even though I ask this of thee
The pain and the ache of the victims I see

And yet O Lord as the killers walk free
The victims' children they walk in fear
The surviving parent is so anxious
A burden now placed on her small shoulders

How do we console in a moment like this
What words to say when a loved one's amiss
Do we just sit and contemplate
On a senseless act that was commit

Show us the way we ask of you
To see the right of the wrong done
Give them the strength to carry on
'Cause Lord they're really broken

A SOLDIER'S TALE

Into the army I must go
To fight for man and country
At a tender age of just sixteen
Untrained for a battle assignment

Guns are issued – bullets too
Orders given – what to do
Drums are beating – men start marching
Into the unknown – I must go

Weapons ready – bugles blowing
The oath of loyalty taken
I must defend one's flag and country
And fight for my fellowmen

With a *rat-tat-tat* and *bang, bang, bang*
Trumpet sounds and men all shouting
The roar of jet engines screams overhead
How many of us will soon lie dead?

A ping and a hit from a sniper's gun
The young man reeled and fell...
Up he gets as he tries to stand tall...
But falls back down as he bled

As he lay there dying, gun in his arms
His sister's face he sees
I'm one man lost in a fight to be free
So sister, do not weep

My life I give as duty bound
And proud of it indeed
For sister dear, I'll lie here dead
But I know that you will be free

A VALENTINE DECLARATION

Valentine's 14th is now here
My love I must declare
As we were told like long ago
These words I write to you

I bless the day that I met you
I bless the night when I lay by you
And as I wake this February morn
My thanks I give for the day you were born

Yours eyes of green, an emerald sheen
Your lips I kiss – each time a wish
Your hair the colour of a sunset's eve
My love for you – a lasting bliss

ABBY-CLARE

I want you to know that since you were born
You were loved by us from day one
You do not know us but we know you
And your face we have never forgotten

With curly blonde hair and your daddy's semblance
A beautiful child – our gift from God
But born out of wedlock, a fuss this has caused
Between two people who should love you the most

A decade's now passed and we wonder how you are
Your parents you see dear, did not see eye to eye
He does take care of you tho' but this you do not know
And every day he speaks to you as you sit there on the wall

The lies and deceit that made our absence clear
And much as we fought were told to stay away
You'll soon be of age tho' and hope you'll find a way
To your blood family lost that was taken away

And when you start to look, dear
You'll find us waiting here
These missing years of love you've lost
We'll pretend they were not there

A welcome with open arms
And all the love that's amiss
To see your face, to hear your voice
Our own sweet Abbey-Claire

AFGHAN SORROW

When war is fought and death is the price
And atrocities made under intense pressure
By those that are trusted and there to protect
And then are called to face 'justice'

Who sent them there in the first instance?
These men and women of such great valour
Where vows are taken to defend and protect
Their own, beloved, country

Another man's land, out to defend
A selfish war they have fashioned
And our brave men and women alike
Will die for a reason they know not why

To look a bullet in the eye
To see torn limbs and hear a baby cry
People's traumatic stares with fallen tears
And then the question is asked – W H Y?

Is it no wonder my heart bleeds
For these men and women – with P T S D
Whose job they did as were duty bound
But now are left but to take account

They're now at home and out the force
Some can't sleep but sit there alone
To hold it together their lives torn apart
With memories brought back from a war they fought

The medals gained now packed away
Their spirit once strong but now is broken
They've done their bit for country and all
But where's their country when these men fall?

AUTUMN LEAVES

Autumn leaves, they just keep falling
A beautiful display they make
And when they do I think of you
And the day they bore you away

I see your face – I kiss your lips
I feel your warmth – the touch of your hair
But as I sit in this old rocking chair
I see you, my love, but you're not here

Oh, autumn leaves as you gently fall
I wish you can hear my plea
For when you're done and the winter's song's in
I wish to be whisked to my darling

BABES OF THE STREET

They live on the streets
And in the alleyways
They live in the sewer
And on the rubbish tips

They're frozen with the cold
They're even petrified
They're often well beaten
Some abused and even killed

The tales they tell are really quite unnerving
Of a mental mother as she goes prostituting
At the age of six – the young boy sells
Sweets to the passing – to make ends well

Another his age is living on the edge
His home is down below in the sewer deep
He'll leave solely to find some food to eat
A pocket he'll pick and hope not to get beat

For another the price is quite high
He allows himself to be abused
For him to survive he must do this
His payment you see, is a small plate of food

As night time arrives they all huddle together
And in their tiny little hands are dirty plastic bags
And the glue inside you'll see them inhale
As this it seems their only means of solace

These little mites are shown the door
By those who could not keep
And so they sleep – a blissful sleep
In their new found home – the street

BEGUILED

In the magic of the still dark night
My soul I will let go and rise
I'll search for joys not of this earth
And forget earth's pains and ire

When dawn approaches, no longer still
I'll be called back down like the whip-poor-will
To once more experience earth's little things
But my thoughts will be with my runaway things

BIBLE IN HER HAND

A mother in her rocker
A bible in her hand
A baby lying in a cradle
Made of wood and sand

A meagre fire burning
Of little peat or coal
A shawl but to keep her warm
In this her wintry home

The cold winds blowing hard
The snow keeps coming down
A mother keeps on rocking
Still bible in her hand

The baby's now awake
And silent is the day
The only sound keeps coming
Is the crying that he makes...

BURNING LOVE

Miles and miles between us
But I was compelled to go
I pray for the sunrise of the new morn
When I'll wing my way home to you

I'm over here and you are there
The moon and dark nights between us
I vision your face and feel a thousand pains
And tears are shed like the heavens when it rains

I miss the feel of your tender touch
The softness of your voice
I long for the taste of your sweet lips
And to feel the heat of your soul

But until then my dearest one
My love I'll pour out and send with the wind
And when I hear the wind does howl
My name I know you are calling out

BY GONE MEMORIES

Oh to be on that dusty gravel road
With the sounds and the clatter of the old horse cart
The hot steamy tropic air but a gentle breeze
The fragrance of the forest green, monkeys climbing trees

Kids off to school so neatly uniformed
Some hitch a lift on rickety old bikes
An acute sense of balance they all show off
Yet arriving at school immaculately clad

The sounds of chatter and of laughter
And sounds of music of different culture
Smells of dukuno and cuk-nut pie
All lovingly baked in a forest fire hearth

Where's this dusty road? you ask yourself
That leads to these wondrous sounds and smells
A tiny little isle in the carib sea
A place I know that's called Belize

BY THE RIVERSIDE

I sit here so quietly – by the riverside
The only sounds to be heard are the noises of the night
The creaking of a branch – the rustling of the leaves
Limbs falling to the ground – and sounds of a beast

I sit here so quietly – by the riverside
New shadows appear with dancing lights
As I lift my head shadows cross my face
Made by whispering trees and the soft moonlight

I sit here so quietly – by the riverside
The smell of the forest in the gentle night air
Nature's aroma – a perfume of its own
Come join me and share the pleasures of this zone

BYSTANDER

When people get robbed and mugged
And left to their demise
Why do we look and stare
But did not interfere?

Why when the victim's pronounced dead
A flurry of questions arises?
Then people wonder about the situation
And if it could have been prevented

Are we a callous cold-hearted nation
And people of no concern?
There's no need for strangeness or belligerence
Or fear of the unknown

When you do find yourself in need
From a passing total stranger
Please lend a hand and just consider
You may prevent a disaster

This may seem rather obvious
And easier said than done
But let's stop being bystanders
And show that we can respond

CANCER

These tiny cells within us
That grow at a quickened pace
Cells we're not aware of
Until a pain is felt

And when we're diagnosed
Of this disease on board
An imminent fear of disbelief is felt
This fear of the unknown

When once we were strong
And now we are weak
The road we now face
A road we must prolong

The chemo and radiation
A challenge of its own
But the worst one of all
Is the look of one's expression

The changes that occurs
Denial some will go
Others will not cope
And rejection some will show

Do not be afraid of this path you're about to take
Know they mean well and prepared they must be
For this they will see of your reaction
Is not from you but from the medication

With this in mind…
A quote if I may…
Cancer is not a sentence
But a phase in one's existence

CHRISTMAS REFLECTIONS

Whatever happened to the spiritual Christmas?
The one we knew and loved
Where the preparation and anticipation
For the coming of 'Christ' is made?

We no more take time to be aware
Of the true meaning of Christmas
As we prepare for worldly things
No memory of 'a child's birth' is there

Whatever happened to the hanging of stockings
At the edge of your baby's bed
All filled with sweets and smelly things
And the joys that Christmas brings?

Instead we hear the children say
At Christmas time – I want
And we the parents go out and get
For fear not to disappoint

Whatever happened to the very connection
Between memory, goodness, and emotion
The purpose of the Advent season
A time for us to reflect on?

COME SACRED SPIRIT

Come Sacred Spirit of fire and love
Come Sacred Spirit – anoint us from above
Your holy gifts on us bestow
The Father and ~The Son we know

Come Sacred Spirit – our souls you rest
In our hearts I beg you stay
Your grace to us I ask you give
For a holy life on earth to live

To all you three be glory given
As you drive our enemy from within
With you by our side and as our guide
Our path is secured in heaven

COME WALK WITH HIM

Come walk with Him in His holy grace
Come walk and share in His blessings
By turning and living by His trust
We'll walk this path to heaven

This Lenten time we look to restore
Our friendship with The Almighty
This forty days of our testing
May the Holy Spirit guide us

Bless us this Lent with your power O Lord
Help us to be true and strong
Our own temptations to face in your name
And all that we do – Amen

CONNED

All these years of toil and stress
For a better way of life
Every brick that's carried and plenty of sacks
The memories come flooding back

Briefcase in hand a stranger came
With a proposal and a plan
A spiel was given for buying my home
The seed already planted for a better one

Now I'm a person of no education
But this home of mine I'm proud of
This buyer he painted a picture so real
I found myself so trilled

With pen in hand he made me sign
A document that sounds so worthy
Next I knew I sold my home
A cheque in hand for 30

I sit here alone with head in my hand
Pondering at my next move
The bank just told me that I've been conned
I should have got 130

CRAZY

The word 'crazy' – what does it mean?
This word that's used in many ways
A word that can be so highly offensive
A word that can be abusive

Am I crazy when I declare my love?
Am I crazy when I do odd things?
Am I crazy when I shout my mouth off?
Am I crazy when I speak out loud?

Crazy-crazy – lack-a-daisy
It's better to be crazy than lazy
Crazy to be in a place like this
Well hell, maybe I am crazy….

DANCE OF THE FIREFLIES

You are known as a fly
But you really are a bug
Your colours are varied
You are yellow, green, or red

Your home is in the marshes
And the wetlands too
With one pair of wings
You fly but very low

You light up in the dark
And a spectacle you make
A dance of unison
A glow-worm composition

Your light portrays a message
A means of warning sign
The one though I love best
Is a call to your lover's nest

I sit here on a quiet night
Reflections in the dark
Enjoying this performance
The dance of the fireflies

DANGERS OF THE SEA

I stood here in the early morn
I feel the warmth of the gentle breeze
I open my eyes and what do I see?
The rising sun a spectacle be

The relaxing sounds of the deep blue sea
The gentle wave as she kisses the shore
The gulls and pelicans fly high above
And the sharks and rays swim below

But on this ocean there is danger abound
From those of crime as they but hound
Holidaymakers who sails out to greet
The wondrous beauty of the deep

Beware my friends, take care, take care
Take care when the sea screams
There's those out there out to prevent
Your decision to execute a dream

Some may live and some may die
By this unlawful piracy act
As they board your boat, a sure known fact
These men with guns and knives

Beware my friends, take care, take care
Take care when the sea screams
There's those out there out to prevent
Your decision to execute a dream

DREAM ON

When we were young and love was sweet
A pledge was made to each other
We knew love and what sweet love
There could have been no other

The years have gone, the kids have flown
And all we do is sit here alone
Our hairs all white – can scarcely walk
And wish the clock would turn back

Now my years are more I dream of packing
You'd never see me again
We once had love but now it's gone
Cannot stay where love's not wanted

Two strangers under this roof
This is what we have become
The wish to spread my wings and fly
But in this state... dream on

ECHOES OF HELL

They are on the streets again
Why they do? – we do not know
Their intent but to kill
To scatter blood and bone

They care not who they hurt
Be it woman, man, nor child
With minds full of fury
A sickness that's gone wild

A country plagued with violence
Is but their intent
Terror is their method
And to paint the streets with red

It's not about you
It's not about me
It's about the person we cannot see
Who's ready to pounce at any time
For whatever means he feels

Who knows how long
Must we live on the edge
In this land that is betrayed
By the governance of its officials
Who live at ease it seems

At this point in time we can affect
The chance we have right now
To right the wrong that is but done
And escape these echoes of hell

FACE IN THE FLAMES

I sit here by the fire mulling over my thoughts
I find myself looking deep at your face
And as my thoughts they turn to you
My tears they just start falling

I watch the colours in the brilliance of the flames
I see autumn leaves and I see your smile
And as it performs a plasmatic dance
I feel your hold and the passion inside

Spellbound I am as I look in the fire
But your face I no longer see
The flames they speak of my uncalled horror
As I sit here and ponder this aching sorrow

FAITH

Devoted Christians we call ourselves
I question the truth in that
In days gone by we abide by the faith
Now we don't, and that's a fact

O for the days when reverence was paid
To the Lord, God the Almighty
Where six days a week we laboured with love
And filled the church on Sundays

But that was then and now is now
And faith there is not many
For in my church this I see
People of hardly any

People of the world I call to you
In your faith you must believe
Dispel these thoughts and images have
Of hypocrisy and greed

The doubt, pretence, and being two-faced
To profane, blaspheme, and swear
Trust and believe in the Lord above
And assurance you will receive

Hypocrisy and Faith
Two words that comes to mind
But which do we call upon
When trials and doubt set in

'O my God, why? – O Dear God – Why?'
We always seem to call on him whenever we please
So think people think, come back to God's domain
Do not let life's troubles dissuade your beliefs

In this life of ours, Faith is first, second, and third
So please Him above and believe in this word
Faith is love, faith is all, faith is all about trust
So this message to you I bring

FAMILY TIES

I sit there and watch amongst all the chatter
Each other speaking in a loud frenzied manner
They laugh and converse at the same time
A nonchalant mannerism but all is just the same

A comment is made from one in the group
A firm sense of falseness distinguished in the voice
A look of annoyance is seen on one's face
A sarcastic remark will then escalate

The start of an argument this is for sure
As all intervenes as sides they procure
Where stands are taken be it right or wrong
All in defence of the opted one

A manner taken – a show of stance
A deliberate show to the impeding one
A message read just keep your distance
You may be blood – but one of us none

Is this an end to family ties
Where love should be strong to the bitter end?
No sides should be taken – no matter as to reasons
A bond that's broken through false allegations

I stare at the faces in this picture of mine
The urge to lash out – I feel I must shout
The emotions felt from an unfinished time
With anger and rage just waiting to come out

I've distanced myself but I can turn this around
An advocate I'll be for misunderstandings felt
An achievement on my own with the ones I know best
And a completion I feel as I lay this to rest

FIRE & RAIN

A place I know when a fire rages
Its people are drawn like bees to honey
No thought is given for one's own safety
Just the need to witness the burning

A place I know when the rain pours down
Its people to cover they run
No thought is given if one gets delayed
It's important they don't get sodden

A place I know where there's fire and rain
And its people's grasp of these elements
Where danger is present in the burning of a flame
And safety is depicted by the pouring of the rain

A place I know where there's fire and rain
A smile it brings to my face
An expression to mind from the locals there
We run to fire – but we run from rain

FOR WHAT?

This way of life, this way of strife
Is it all very worthwhile?
The blood that's shed, the sweat and tears
War, for what?

The way to thrive, to stay alive
A must I ask myself
The many men their lives they lost
For what, for what?

Blood, sweat, tears, they gave
For conflict of man's own making
Peace they say, not war, not war
Yet war don't lead to peace

At the end of war what do we see
Men alive with question eyes
Back with memories that will remain
For what, for what?

FORGOTTEN DREAMS

When I was young
Many a dream had I
Nothing much to regret
Most of them forgot

But when I think of the past
A smile it crosses my face…
It slowly turns to a frown
Then to a point of no going back

It's all to do with memories you see
Some you can't erase
For years and years of festering
Within my living essence

A bit of reflection of horrors past
This path I must dispel
I will not ride with forgotten dreams
Nor the devil to take my soul

Sad memories are a bad thing
It eats at your very being
So talk out loud – shout it out
Those who are still dreaming

GHOSTS

Many and varied the ghosts that are supposed
To haunt our country's shores
It may be a street or a silent lane
Or even an open field

They appear on the land or even the sea
And places that are neglected
Whilst others frequent busy sites
Like even a super market

A sensation of coldness is always around
A portrayal of a ghostly presence
So watch how you go for you never know
Who is standing there in attendance

GRASP OF THE UNKNOWN

Here one minute, then not
A feel of emptiness...
The many faces that I see...
But then I know them not

Where am I going, I ask myself?
I've absolutely no idea...
How long have I been experiencing this
This sort of 'emptiness'?

I'm disoriented and so confused
I feel I've woken up
I look around but I'm in a daze
I can't believe this madness

This awareness of ignorance
Is just not funny no more
It's really rather scary
This grasp of the unknown

HAPPINESS

Happiness is the smile when I see your face
The feel of your love, your warmth, your embrace

Happiness is our children when I hear them laugh
To see the muck on their face, to wipe away their tears

Happiness is our lives and all the positive things
The music and the songs, and everything they bring

HEAVEN

What words are there but to describe
Heaven's beauty to be seen and know
Are there colours, angels, prayers, and songs
Or the magic of a double rainbow

What words are there but to describe
Heaven's beauty as we know it
The look on the faces of little children
Of joy, delight, and elation

The faces of people – a glowing light
A show of immense pleasure
The trees, the meadows, the clouds, and skies
To earth an exquisite measure

For heaven there is a price to pay
And this was shown to us
He that died on the cross for men
And from the dead he rose

Heaven is worth waiting for
And when you're there – you'll see
So put your trust in the Creator's love
And live in the fullness of He

HELL'S BELLS

As I drove up this lonely road
My eyes they did but see
Amid the bushes there I spy
A timid boy lie he

Why do you hide my little one?
And why do you cower so?
Please sir, said he, please don't tell
I must not hear that bell

My father he but drinks all day
I live a life of hell
His message to me is when he needs
He'll always ring that bell

I make his tea, I fetch his drink
I even wash his face
I do these things and even more
That I'm beginning to abhor

And while he drinks I will not sleep
For sure that bell he'll ring
I just can't do this anymore
You see, he'll call for more

So run away I must and go
For fear of what I know
If I stay, sir, I will be dead
For that I am but sure

And as I stare and looked at him
I can but feel his horror
For in his eyes there I see
Are little tears of sorrow

I thank you for your kindness, sir
But me you did not see
I must be bound and a new life found
And escape the likes of he

HIGHWAY TO PERDITION

My young friend, she walks the streets
Her clothes all ragged and torn
With eyes that stare as in a trance
A wistful and pitiful expression

A tale she'll tell of wretchedness
A tale full of glumness
A life she led from an early age
A life full of sadness

Her parents are drug users
And always on a high
They'll send her out late at nights
To pay for their obsession

Her body's used so many times
She feels so impaired
If bruises were an extra skin
This coat she'll surely wear

Her head she'll not hold high
Her face she'll keep well hidden
To veil the beatings she received
To feed her parents' addiction

How long must she continue
On this ungodly road
Where love and respect pass her by
On this highway of perdition?

HOW FAR YOU'VE FLOWN

How far you've flown my feathered winged friend
As your chest heaves high and low
I bet you've come from a country far
And thousands of miles I'm sure

Over the distance you have flown
To get away from the cold
And all through the air you sing a song
As this journey you took on

And now you've come this far my friend
I hope you've found your place
For this a must, a time for rest
To lay your head upon your weary breast.

HOW LONG?

I lie here in bed
A gun shot to my chest
A means not of my making
An explanation not worth taking

Recovery is a dream
As I lay here paralyzed
You see my condition
Is slowly deteriorating

Sometimes I do well
Sometimes I do bad
But this time I'm down
And there's no going back

My body, it's like in pieces
All broken up like glass
I'm to stay in one position
As I take in the situation

I pray to the father and ask his help
For the good things I have done
I ask him for forgiveness
And that is keeping me strong

How long you ask will I lie here?
How long is a piece of string?
This condition I wish you not
But Hope I too must cling

HOW LOW IS LOW?

In the heat of the day they walk and trudge
So sure of themselves, so shamelessly smug
The look on their face, don't mess with me
Beware my appearance or you go through me

A modern teen world of our young children
With pants hanging low, a modern trend
It does not matter the disturbance cause
While the younger generation point and pause

Agitated parents ponder in shock
They tell the law but they don't react
The answers they say to the reason why
Will make you cringe and want to cry

If you're bold enough and talk about it
They look at you and laugh out loud
And actions then taken to show the lot
It's cool they say, try to dress this way

If only they knew of their ridiculous look
With pants hanging low below their butt
A positive show of complete self-worth
Is the message sent that is coming forth

It's indecent, immoral, offensive and lewd
It's wrong, improper, and so uncouth
A bad example of how low is low
This message that is sent to our innocent youths

I SING A SONG

This song I sing for you to listen
So please don't fly away
Sweetly a song that wings through the air
I sing, I sing just for you

I look at you and all I see
Sweet summers kiss and a taste of wine
Your angel's eyes and strawberry lips
My angel delight, you're mine

My song is sung and now you're gone
I watch you fly in the bright summer's sun
I make a plea to the light of the day
To keep you safe until you return

I sing a song for you to listen
I sing but you do not hear
That day you flew into the summer's sun
You gave no sign – was that the time?

JESUS' BIRTH

The night is cold and jingle bells ring
Around the tree we all will sing
The candles are lit, our hands are joined
This blessed night – this clear midnight

O Silent Night – O Holy Night
O Come All Ye Faithful
Christians awake – salute this morn
And the birth of our Lord Emmanuel

O Little Town of Bethlehem
You're different now than then
Where war and strife has played their part
And peace on earth is not

To all good people of this earth
I beg of you, consider
He that came and died for us
And heed the message sent

Shout you people, Shout!
Sing out and raise your voice
Throughout the mayhem of this world
Shout out the name of the Lord

So sing my people sing
Like the herald angels sing
Peace and goodwill this Christmas time
Sing praises to our King

JUNGLE RAPE

They enter our country like spirits of the night
An illegal invasion not of our delight
Their one intent our heritage to take
For a better way of life they say to make

A country so small – yet so tall
It's woodland of trees, mahogany and all
Where wildlife live, all different kinds
The scarlet macaws the most exotic of all

But then they come with machetes and guns
Our trees they hacked till they all fall down
Our scarlet macaw is now deteriorating
As they feast on our bird with much liking

Our country's mahogany – our cherished hardwood
Our birds and beasts and all that's preserved
Our artefacts from the Mayan's gone
Pilfered and stolen with no concern

Like jaguars they creep and rape in the night
Our forests and jungle as we sleep
So come on people, let's defend and fight
Them that's destroying our heritage rights

KEEP ON LOOKING

Before you decide to go
Remember what you're leaving
That this is of your making
You're the one that's done the cheating

Your love for me is no more
Then just go out that door
To your new love of just a while
And feed her with your lies

You say I'm to blame
For things I did not do
I tried to comprehend
This change in you

The guilt you are portraying
Was brought on by yourself
The lives you're destroying
Is not just one but many

So just before you go
Don't think of coming back
For she will find out as I did
That she's the third in line

This silly game you're playing
You think is just quite fitting
I don't know what you're hunting for
But I know you'll keep on looking

LADY D & D

A story to be told
Of a perfect fairy-tale
A marriage of two lovers
A Prince and his Lady

A marriage of grandeur
A marriage of splendour
A marriage full of joy
But one destined for sorrow

A broken accordance
Of betrayal unbound
A marriage separation
And a Lady's depression

A new love she has found
The old one is forgotten
But not by those out there
For their constant attention

Then one dark night
The hand of fate stepped in
The Lady and her new love
In heaven a life begin

The memories of these two
Will always come to mind
As true love they have found at last
But always they were hound

LOOK HIM IN THE EYE

Who can look death in the eye
And say it is all right
When our deepest fears we see?

Who can look death in the eye
And say it is all right
When our greatest fears are nigh?

My body I find is lying still
As weird thoughts play their part
I'm in a maze in a very dark space
Can't find my way to the start

Is this the path we all must take
As we make way for the new?
And as this chill bears over me
This door I'll close and...

LOOKING FOR YOURSELF

You scheme against others
You cheat and you conspire
Yet when challenged with this matter
You're always full of flatter

Your walk is of a proud stance
Your voice so silky smooth
Your smile full of charm
No cheat would look like you

To know you as a charlatan
To know you as a fraud
The skills you profess you have
But these you do not have

You hide behind these traits
These wonderful values of life
Why don't just be yourself?
But this you don't know how

Take time to find yourself
Find out what you can accomplish
You had your cause for all these flaws
Now allow yourself your merit

People will like you and some people won't
It does not matter if they do or don't
Listen to your inner self and boost your self-esteem
For when these qualities you have found, a nicer person be

LOST LOVE

The first time I saw your face
Something inside me stopped
Your look, your smile, your eyes said it all
I had to answer your silent call

You took my hand and then we dance
I felt I was floating on air
I felt so safe, I felt so warm
When I was in your arms

And then as quick as you came
Just as quickly you were gone
A touch of the hands, a parting kiss
And I was left here alone

The years have passed, decades since
But your face I see so often
I'm married now, and so are you
But you were always the one

MALICIOUS BEING

You called me – you called me
But why did you call me?
You never liked me
You hated me
Now you call me

You want to be my friend you say
Why now – why now?
I've put up with your jibes and jeers
And kept on my merry way

You tell them I'm your best pal
Although it's costing me
Whenever we go out together
The bills they come my way

I know I'm idiotic and sometimes thick
But why should the likes of you
For your self-satisfaction my imperfection
Use me with your nasty tricks?

MANY A BRIDGE

Many a bridge I have to cross
As my spirit's down – and I can't go on
I can't understand – I'm at a lost
Oh but to be found

Many a bridge I have to cross
To save this soul of mine
For years I chose a path to dread
And times I wish me dead

Many a bridge I have to cross
To find this Saviour of mine
For him to show the way to me
And experience his love divine

MEMORIES SO DARK

No matter where or why
No matter what the season
It always seems so dark
And always without good reason

It's been so many years ago
A prisoner of war I was
I thank the Lord that I'm alive
But some did not survive

And as I sit here all alone
A frail old man of ninety-two
I see myself at twenty-two
With a pick and shovel in hand

That path in life I did not tell
Of the torment and horrors felt
And then the memories they start come back
Of a young man's torture in an old man's head

An angry man, a bitter man
A man who can't forget
Just sitting old and all forlorn
With his memories and the dark

MESSAGES IN A POEM

When feelings are illustrated
In words of prose or verse
When words are read and bring to mind
Perhaps an account of woe

When feelings are depicted
In words of rhyme or ode
When thoughts are brought to one's mind
Perhaps of a call for aid

How many that used this method
How many that used this style
To send a message contained within
Written words of prose and verse?

MESSAGES ON A TREE

Etched in the bark of an ageing tree
Many a message to examine
A tree that became a secret friend
In the glimpse of one's own legend

The messages tell of yearning for love
With pictures of faces and beasts
Pictures of hearts and carved initials
And pictures of someone's needs

A depiction of love and loneliness
Or maybe a cry of help...
These messages that's written on a tree
For those who find to see

MONKEY SEE – MONKEY DO

Children are so lovely
In expressing their views
Things that come naturally
In everything they do

A fact to behold
A sort of adulation
They latch on to something
A cat, a tree, a person

A show they'll put on
Of mimicry and joy
A walk in mom's heels
A sight to consider

It's time now for dinner
And her manners she forgot
As head over plate
She's eating like the cat

I can go on and tell
Of her impish deeds and do's
A very true example of
'Monkey see' – 'monkey do'

MIRROR OF VANITY

I look in the mirror and what do I see?
A picture of you looking back at me
I stare at your face – a beautiful face…
I talk to you – and you to me

I look in the mirror and what do I behold?
A beautiful maiden just 16 years old
A show of passion in her expression
With pouting red lips and rounded hips

My household mirror my much-loved friend
You tell me what I need to know to the bitter end
They may think I'm vain – but then that's my game
For the fairest of all is this young dame

MY BROTHER

As I sit here and wonder
My thoughts turn to you
The games we played
And that song you sang – my brother

And all the fighting and in-betweens
And disagreements in our teens
The tales you told and the jokes you played
And you just laughed – my brother

You made me laugh, you made me cry
You even helped to make me lie
But when I ache and I am hurting
You're always there – my brother

We've all grown up and there you go
Our sisters' homes you'll visit
A daily routine this you do
A must in your daily list

Across the seas I think of you
And all these years of missing you
A special love I have for you
My one and only brother

(This is dedicated to my only brother 'John' with fondest love.)

MY FRIEND

Why do you sit there in the dark?
Your head you hang down low
That look on your face – one of pain
And the lines, the lines they show

Who are you that sits in the dark
Your eyes so widely open
That probes the shadows of the night?
I wonder, what's in your sight?

Your voice, your voice, as you mumble to yourself
A discussion with whom I question
Your hands, you just keep wringing them
A message of 'desperation'?

How is it you have ended up here?
For sure you weren't this way
You once were a man of great esteem
And now you walk as... in a dream

My friend, I wish I could help to find
A way to bring you back
From one who seems to have lost his soul
To one who was once in... control

MY GHOSTLY FACE SEE

I sit here in my chair
I saw him standing there
No words come from his mouth
My thoughts are why you're there

20 minutes I sat, 20 minutes stood he
And still no greeting came
The thought that sits there in my mind
Is, I wonder what's your game?

Up I stood to get a drink
And in the house I went
And then an almighty bang
And then I fell down dead

My killer was but just a lad
Who preyed on elders it seems
Too lazy to go and fend for himself
They rob and kill for greed

I've seen his face but no one else has
No earthly justice he'll face
I'll come back from the grave, and he
Forever my ghostly face see

MY GUIDING LIGHT

Twinkle, twinkle, little star
Way up high and oh so afar
With your light you guide me through
This dark path throughout the night

Twinkle, twinkle, little star
My life, my joy, my child so fair
Your laugh, your smile, your gentle cry
To you I'll sing a lull-a-bye

Twinkle, twinkle, little star
You're my friend, I know you are
There are times I don't see you
But I know you're always there

Twinkle, twinkle, little star
You're around and you're so rare
Keep continue shining bright
I'll always find you my guiding light

MY HANDSOME BUTTERFLY

You're black and brown, green and blue
With wings so beautifully coloured
You flutter and dance so daintily
A ballet of exquisite pleasure

You kiss the flowers
You smell the grass
You quiver through the air
No noise you make while you portray
A beautiful silent sonata

You are a vision my winged flutter by
A prayer I whisper to you
To take with you as you fly through the air
My handsome butterfly

MY MOTHER

I would not be here if not for her
I would not be here at all
I am so glad I'm of her genes
My beautiful, beautiful, mother

The pictures I see of her in mind
As she sits to stitch our clothes
The care she took while she does
And all the time she sings

Her voice is of an angel's choir
So beautifully sang a song
No other has a voice like her
She's a lovely coloratura

Another picture comes to mind
Is that of her in the yard grounds
With rake in hand she will make smart
And produce a heavenly garden

And every Thursday there's a treat
As that's the day she gets paid
We always have that 'arctic roll'
Somehow she thinks we deserved it

But Christmas is the best of all
As she replaces the old with the new
And all these things she made herself
Then gives the old to the poor

MY ROSE

A single rose you placed in my hand
A symbol of love untainted
Its scent a fragrance so bitter sweet
A subtle shade of deep blood red

My rose and I, we tell each day
Of this special love so right
A vow we make our love will last
And never to expire

And then one day my beautiful rose
Its thorns drew blood of mine
I watched it wilt, wither, and die
And wonder, has my true love died?

MY SISTER SAID

Your poems are so sad
You write of painful moments
And of hostile times gone by

My sister said to me one day
Of happier times please write
But how can I when happy thoughts
Evade my head – try as I might

I think not of myself
Or those I grew up with
I think but of my children
And their way of life now in

Two different worlds theirs and mine
This way of life we live
One of blissful 'freedom'
One of pure 'restriction'

So do I write of joys gone by
Or write of my children's woes
To bring awareness of these afflictions
On them we have bestowed?

I write about these actions
For others to study
To see the harm that we have done
To those that we love dearly

So sister dear, I wish I could
Write something of bliss
But change must come to the fore
In this nation our child lives in

So until then we can but hope
For them to find back 'freedom'
That's been destroyed by many a man
And free them from 'restriction'

So until then I will still pen of these deplorable deeds
I must bring them to the fore for others to see
It has to stop, I know not how, but write I know I must
And fight back for their freedom and dispel of this unjust

(For my sister Teri.)

MY SON

It does not seem so long ago
Since you were my little boy
You who filled my life so much
With so, so many joys

Now here you are, my little grown man
And I ask you to remember
Be fair and share and always care
And realise who you are

You're kind, you're sweet, you're a gentleman
You always put others first
I found that in you as I watched you grow
And so very proud – my son

And now you're off to pastures new
As you leave I'll try not to cry
Just once more son – I'd like to say
You will always be my little boy

MY TRANQUIL MOON

Where are you my tranquil moon?
I wish for you to appear
Will you not turn your face to mine
As I look for you who is so divine?

I need to wash the dirt of this earth
In the radiance of your light
Before my entry to the unknown
So present yourself this night

I find the days are getting cold
My bones they are so old
My hair's all white and I barely walk
And my eyes can't see in the dark

Won't you come and see my loneliness?
I'm someone of no existence
And when the snow begins to fall
My spirit floats free in your brilliance

MY VALENTINE

I don't need to go to the moon
Or dance amongst the stars
I just need to be with you
For I love you as you are

We've been together quite a while
The wind beneath our wings
My love you've been all this time
My darling 'Valentine'

'NO' – TO OFFSHORE DRILLING

We in Belize are saying 'No' to off-shore drilling
It's clearly plain to see the government wants no telling
An intricate issue of a very serious nature
Where eco risks and energy levels 'not to discuss' a matter

People of Belize, I ask of you – open your eyes and see
What God has given you and yours and for all others to see
Beautiful clear seas, a marine world of its own
Of coral reefs and deep-sea life, a gift, our very own

Whether to drill or not is a multilateral question
Of political autonomy and ecological reasons
A threat to our waters and protection of our shores
That's what I see of corporations likely to bore

And if they drill as known in the past, no safety measures in place
This will only come to light, when calamity has transpired
Pollution from drilling, oil spills from lines and tankers
Our land and infrastructure – a sure planned man disaster

So people of Belize get up – get up and defend your rights
Keep all these planned investors right out of our sights
Remember oil and water, they just do not blend
Remember our sea mammals and how our wildlife fend

Remember too this black gold, they just might not find
And when this has happened, they'll leave this land behind
And all the damage done that they have created
Is left with us to be hated for tens and tens of decades

Shout 'No' to offshore drilling – shout out loud and clear
For those who do not listen – you must make them hear
This is our seas – a blessing of our own
No man must come in and for their greed destroy our soul

NOSY BUSY BODIES

You can't let others be – can you?
You always have to gossip
Why must you always interfere?
Are you that fed up – REALLY?

Why not go out and find a chore
Instead of making conflict?
If you're that old, find a hobby
Or go and do some gardening

What people do with their lives
Is their own concern
There's no reason for you to intrude
Just get on with your own

You nosy busy bodies
You have nought better to do
Stop prying on my situation
Just go and work on your own

NOT YET

Not yet – not yet
It's always – not yet
Why are we so negative?
Why can't we be positive?

Whenever asking a question
It's always 'not yet'
When will it be 'yet'?
It's always in the waiting

These words of 'not yet' you'll find
Can be a cry of plea
For when one's in the passing
You'll hear 'not yet' – 'not yet'

O GLORIOUS BELIZE

O glorious Belize, land of sea and sun
A vow I make to thee
Your people will stand steadfast and strong
To build a nation united and free

Grant us your blessings O God and King
On this land of hope and glory
To honour and defend, far and wide
The name of my country 'Belize'

The flag we fly so proud, so high
Our Coat of Arms so right
Tyrants and despots shall fear the wrought
Of this country's power and might

March on for freedom O people of Belize
Through storm, fire, and prayer
With help from St Michael from heaven above
The road to freedom lies there

God bless this nation one and all
A legacy from a battle fought
This coral land with blue lagoons
Belize O glorious Belize

O SYRIA O SYRIA

O Syria O Syria
What have you done?
Your children are lying
There dead on the ground

Young as we are
We can't seem to follow
The sense of your anger
Against people and all

O Syria – O Syria
Our lives are too young
The love for our country
Must be true and strong

Stop shedding our blood
Wipe away our tears
Teach us a new meaning
Of love, not warfare

O Syria – O Syria
It's time to rethink
An end to this madness must be realized
Peace in our time, is what we desire
O Syria. O Syria, My Syria

REMEMBER PEACE & LOVE

Remember the 1960's
A decade to remember
A time of peace, a time of war
A memorable age to consider

A time two countries raced for space
For fear of the Russian takeover
A time for show of civil rights
And a time for Vietnam

A time where skirts were way up high
And then they were way down low
A time when man walked on the moon
And a time for rock-n-roll

There's Mark Luther King 'I have a Dream'
And people on the picket line
And then you have the Ku Klux Klan
Music, fashion, and hippies

The Beatles group reigned supreme
Their rock fest just drew millions
The hippies with their LSD
And a show of revival response

And as our children played unhurt
Our doors were left wide open
The 60's was a time of change
A time of liberation

QUE SERA SERA

Times when you think you can
You find yourself go wrong
No truer words describe it all
As – Que Sera – Sera

Times when you want to please
For you to be recognized
But then you lose that recognition
Again – Que Sera – Sera

You try so hard – you try to please
You've always got to succeed
It does not matter – fail or achieve
Que Sera – Sera

Times like these a lesson to learn
Don't expect something in return
Live your life – just for yourself
Que Sera – Sera

UNORTHODOX TEENS

Children born to us, our own flesh and blood
But in their youthful faces we throw dirt and mud
Through a time of puberty, joy, and emotion
A time when they need us most and an explanation?

We leave them on their own, too busy with our intentions
From us their parents there seems no intervention
But when mistakes they make, we call them names
And we but have no shame for a name that extremely hurts

These rebel children go on a task of what they should be
But in their heads they realise these names they're called is he
With this in mind, things they do bring them to the law
The one aim but to prove their worth, for want of recognition

These sad young teens act their thoughts of what they should be
Portrayed so aggressively to hide their sensitive needs
Still searching for approval the only way they know
While suffering so silently in their world of feeling low

R E D

We see it but a colour – its uses are of many
The blush of an elegant rose, the shade of a cold – your nose
A method of expression, of anger and of passion
Words to always dread, when one says 'I see red'

A show of power known when laying the 'red' carpet
For royal and formal occasions, and those of heads of state
Of happiness a meaning, of joy and elation
Decors of 'red' for some a means of fortune

Warnings are important in the show of signs of 'red'
As notice is drawn, to crisis and those of threat
One I like best of all the colour of my Heart
The colour of my blood as it pumps in and out

So when you see 'red' in any shape or form
Think of its significance and the joy it represents
Enjoy in its beauty and in all our surrounds
And heed her in her warnings when the colour 'red' is shown

REDEMPTION TIME

Belize, my wonderful Belize
You once were a beautiful land
But now my tears I shed
For you I do but cry

The horror that bleeds us dry
The unease that runs in our blood
Where freedom once is now but gone
O Belize I do but cry

People of no protection are we
Who now reside in fear
How did we become this way
O Belize, I ask you why?

You don't hear me when I call you out
My cries they go unheard
Your children hunt each other down
Like beasts out in the wild

Belize, my beautiful Belize
Pain is all I feel
O for you to rise again
I must believe, Belize

SHE

Standing on the shore – a vision I see
A woman of love and beauty
Her hair just wafting in the breeze
A goddess – I do believe

Slowly she walked – towards me she came
Transfixed was I – I feel so insane
And then a voice – a heavenly voice
And then she spoke her name

Her voice is as an angel cry
Her smell is of a rose
Her laugh is delicate as a song
I can but whisper her name

With this she-devil I will walk
As she lures me with her song
Of the treasures, the powers of the sea itself
This She-Devil – she

SORRY DAD

How long has it been since I left you
How long – how long?
My defender in shining armour
My guardian – my Dad

How long has it been since I saw your face?
Too long – too long
A face I knew that once was smooth
I believe now riddled with lines

The years spent with my new found folk
The years forgot of my own blood folk
And now because they've left the nest
The thoughts to you they rest

I so regret it's taken this long
And I wonder how you are
I'm winging my way back to you
To once more be in your arms

How long has it been since I left I ask?
It seems forever long
'Cause now I'm back but you're not there
I'm just too late – I'm just too late

SWEET DREAMS

I dream a dream
A wonderful dream
I held you in my arms
I felt all your charms

I dream a dream
A wonderful dream
We fly and fly
Way up to the sky

I dream a dream
A wonderful dream
Emotions we feel
But I know they're not real

I dream a dream
Such sweet dreams
If only they were real
If only they were real

TEARS OF OUR LADY

O blessed Mother Mary – hear my cry
Help me to please understand
The actions of your children on earth
And as to their reasons why

O Blessed Lady I see you cry
And I can feel your pain
The tears you shed for your son Jesus
And now for us you ache

O Blessed Madonna show us the way
Make us stop this fighting
Teach us the way of the truth and the light
And stop your tears from falling

THARINE RUDON

A woman I knew for many a year
A woman greatly admired
A 'pioneer' for sure, grand by all accounts
Respected and loved by her peers

A lady she was of much status
As her lifelong tale is told
As major roles in society played
And the colourful life she led

Many a love she had and shown
An affiliation with God and country
Music being the core of her manner
Herself – a grand pianist

Her greatest love of all is known
Is that of her political beliefs
And this was clearly made and shown
When speaking of her country Belize

Pioneering in the forming of the PUP
The Peoples United Party...
With other famed patriots the NIP...
The National Independence party

A key role played in the first City Council
Her role in the Workers' Union
And all the time, finesse was shown
As these she did with allegiance

Tharine Rudon to some is known
As 'Thar' or even 'Rudonski'
Among those patriots present and past
For the love she had for her country

For all the work that she has done
To her memory I give recognition
For the huge part played in striving to make
Belize – a better nation

THE ALPHA & THE OMEGA

The Alpha the First – The Omega the Last
A title that's applied both to God and Christ
Some will assess and some will guess
Whether in fact they're the start or end

The Alpha the First – The Omega the Last
Two letters of the Greek Alphabet
A symbol to remind us that God's all eternal
An appearance in Roman Cathedrals

To know the Alpha – to know the Omega
You must understand God's work
His plan on earth but to save us all
A plan He'll see to the end

The Alpha and The Omega, a mystery to us all
But this I do recommend
God does not expect us to understand
But your trust in him I commend

THE APPLE TREE

Deep down in the valley is a place so beautiful
A place of enchantment, a place so peaceful
Everything's so quiet, everything's so green
All you can hear is the waft of the breeze

Sometimes you hear the song of a thrush
Or singing to itself is the stream and its rush
I sit under the shade of the apple tree
And smell the fragrance and this I see

The insects pollinate their place of abode
Then I'm lulled in a dream with the wind and their drone
A man of my dreams he sat beside me
And a song so gently he sang to me

He told of his love so gentle and sweet
As I held his hand our lips then meet
The warmth of his love then fades away
As the chill of the air sets down upon me

I'll leave this place but only for now
My apple tree my secret he'll keep
When tomorrow comes my lover I'll meet
When I dream once more under the apple tree

THE DARK

The daylight fades
New shadows fall
The tiniest of lights
Twinkle in the night

I'm walking so silent
I'm breathing so soft
As I search with my eyes
I listen with my ears

In the calm of the dark
Just the sigh of the breeze
No noise I can hear
No sounds in the air

This in-depth study
Stimulates my mind
But all to be heard
Is the beating of my heart

THE DEVIL'S DOMAIN

The fires – the fires – the fires of hell
A place where some will go
For the evil deeds that we have done
And 'regret' not wanting to know

The smells – the smells – the aroma of hell
Where the devil feasts on our souls
Repent – repent – and avoid this domain
And the devil – he'll feed no more

THE DISABLE ABLE

James' body is all twisted
His speech is sort of droll
Some people laugh at him
The result of an accident roll

Sue has a disturbing impairment
She applied for government aid
An investigation is on-going
A 'cheat' they believe not worth aiding

David's face is covered
He hides the scars he bears
He was a victim of an acid attack
And bears the name of 'Mask Man'

Pete has no legs and sits all day
On a plank of wood with wheels
They got blown off while he fought a war
His hands are now his feet

Your sneers and jeers they want you to know
Are all but classed as mindless
They all were able once, you know
And hope you don't end up like this

THE ELUSIVE HAPPY EVENT

To pen a poem I was asked
Depicting a happy occasion
I wracked my brains and thought it out
For this elusive happy event

I looked back to the start of the year
And what comes to mind
Horrors that got my attention
And wonder to the reason main

War and strife, politics and strikes
What's there to be happy about?
Rape and looting, rioting including
Families evicted through lack of earnings

Hurricanes, tornados, floods and famine
Natural disasters that cause mayhem
Soldiers dying in foreign nations
Leaving young loved ones behind

Tsunamis, earthquakes, mines detonating
Machine guns blazing, bombs exploding
People dying – for what reason
For what I ask myself?

Our children alone can't walk the streets
For sure they'll be attacked
We're prisoners in our own environment
In this world of our own making

So what have I found to be happy about?
Nothing, I'm afraid and that's a fact
We need to change the way we live
And stop living in the devil's domain

So teach our children right from wrong
Teach them of respect
Teach them of family values and worth
Then 'happiness' will come about

With this in mind – I may locate
The illusive happy thought
That has evaded us this time
But is there for our children to find

THE EYES BUT SEE

You make me see the light
You make me see to write
You're there to shed my tears
When I'm down and all forlorn

From the moment I wake
You start to operate
And you stay that way
Till I take on sleep

You take in all around you
The colours, shapes, and sizes
You simply are amazing
This job so awe-inspiring

This brilliant world of ours
Through you it comes to us
The beauty that you show
The colours of your eyes

Without you, I wonder
What I would see
Will my mind I have to use
And see when I sleep?

THE FEATHER

If by you a feather falls
Catch it if you can
A sign of new beginnings
Is sent into your hands

If by you a feather falls
Catch it if you can
This is but a sign of hope
To send away your qualms

If by you a feather falls
Catch it if you can
You are sent good fortune
And this is not per chance

THE FLAMBOYANT TREE

When I was young and quite naïve
A tree my mother planted
A tree she nursed so tenderly
A tree she loved so fondly

She always sat under its shade
A look of peace upon her face
Who would think a love would find
Between a tree and a woman

The day then came she passed away
Her beautiful tree pined and wasted
To tend its branches no one cared
No one seemed to bother

The day came for a new home scheme
The flamboyant tree is in the way
A whirr of the saw and down it came
To make way for another

But I don't care that this has happened
For a new flamboyant is up and growing
Albeit in another place...
For my lovely, lovely, mother

THE FORGOTTEN WINGS

They fly as high as any man
And were called for a 'special role'
To free male pilots for combat duty
In the conflict of World War II

Hundreds of women applied to join
As they took the oath for country
Each was issued a pilot's permit
All trained and passed for duty

Their mission is but to fly aircrafts
From factories to military stations
This they did with the greatest of passion
To free male pilots for war obligations

Many of these women their lives they lost
For services rendered to the war
Through mishaps whilst training on active duty
In an endeavour to support their cause

There's many a heroine who goes unnoticed
And many have been forgotten
And such is the case of the 'forgotten wings'
Who gave their all for their nation

THE FOUR CHAPLAINS

Young and fearful they boarded the ship
This luxury liner turned battle cruiser
Out to defend the land of their birth
Across the seas until it's over

The many dangers there lay ahead
The perils of the sea alone
Where raging waters and ice that flows fast
And the force of the strong gale winds

Packed head to toe way down below
A human sea of doubt and fear
Men in need of a shoulder to lead on
Men in need of hope

But on that ship there's four special men
All men of the cloth
And as they look at the faces of fear
The need for their 'Chaplains' they saw

No care was paid to their title given
Whether Rabbi, Jew, or Reverend
As all knelt with a hymn and a prayer
And a moment of strength was given

Another cold and windy night
A new day now approaching
But in the distance the arm of the enemy
And a command was given to 'fire'

The face of death reached out at the men
On the decks of the battle cruiser
A blinding explosion – a massive destruction
And the cries of pain – the reaction

In the chaos that followed these four special men
Their voices of 'calm' could be heard
To bring peace and hope to panic and unease
As the cruiser start sinking beneath the sea

In less than an hour water covered the deck
As the Chaplains worked against time
But time ran out for these four special men
The last of the life jackets – gone

The ship's demise is almost complete
But at the railings can be seen
Four special men, their arms all linked
As their watery grave they meet

These four special men, all of the 'Cloth'
All of different opinions
But the strength they found in their beliefs
As they made their journey to heaven

THE JEWEL

On high the sweet birds sings
Ripples of a stream gently splash the shore
The whispers of the trees as the wind blows through
While the rays of the sun cast a rainbow below

So dare I love this land of dreams
Of blue lakes and coral reefs
Of silver seas and tropical breeze
This fine-looking isle of exotic trees...

So why do I cry my much loved jewel
Why do I cry for you
The love I once had just for you
Now seems to have turned to hate

My spirit is now broken
And I do ask your pardon
For it cannot be mended
Now my country's robbed and beaten

We have no time to talk but only time to dread
As all our laws are broken and many abroad have fled
I cry for my people and of the customs gone
But I'll just keep on hoping – for the day when again we're one

THE LENTEN SEASON

The day of the ashes – the beginning of Lent
An invite to the altar we're called
The ashes the priest places on our brow
The shape of the cross he makes

And as he does these words he spoke
'For dust you are and dust you'll return'
A symbol of death, a symbol of grief
And a symbol for one's atonement

The day of the ashes – the beginning of lent
A time for prayer and repentance
By our Saviour Lord for us to be cleansed
An undertaking for us to do our best

So Lord I ask, teach us to fast
How to ward off sin and indulging in repast
But make us enjoy the abstinence made
And partake in the hope of obtaining grace

And through these Lenten days, my Lord
I think of your agony and pain
The passion of the cross and that journey made
When you died to save us from sin

And when this season draws to an end
I rejoice at the thought of your resurrection
To once again partake in your rising
On that blessed Easter Morning

THE LETTER 'A'

In days of yore the sin of adultery
Is but a serious crime
If a woman finds herself in this state
A penalty she'll endure by death

A lady once faced the court
As she cradled the babe to which she gave birth
She was so calm, she walked so tall
A sort of elegance showed to one and all

The glaring and the staring she tolerated
As she gently caressed her sweet baby child
And the secret of her lover she would not disclose
But this child she knew, was hers, and hers to keep

The court took pity – a price she had to pay
A public penance she would endure
The letter 'A' placed upon her bosom
The show of a woman who was made 'impure'

Time passed by – her child she had raised
Whilst supporting herself with needle and mend
The glaring and the staring – it is no more
For respect was found in that 'A' she wore

THE MANY FACETS OF LOVE

How many times is the word 'love' used
And in what situation?
'Love for one's country' for example
How is that being shown?

We talk about love for our profession
But what are we really implying?
Then there's the love for our parents
And the love for one's companion

There's love for one's child
A sure significance
And the love for one's God
Depicting assurance

Love between man and woman
Where body and soul are joined
A feeling of pure sensation
A feeling of obsession

But the word 'love' at the end of the day
Is it a single representation?
Can this one symbolic meaning
Be applied to things wide ranging?

THE NAILING & THE RISING

I look at my world today, compared it to the past
We are no different now than it was of then
Tales that are told and how they dealt with an offence
Stories that today are of no consequence

The price one will pay for speaking your mind
The price one will pay for freedom of speech
The price that was paid for trying to educate
One man did such and his life was the rate

Today is not so different though
We speak our minds so harshly
This is shown through other ways
While hurt and maim is the game

Bottles are thrown, bricks are flung
Cars are set on fire
And as we speak, the innocent get hurt
And they didn't even speak

THE NORTHERN LIGHTS

A spectacle to behold on a clear dark night
Are the Northern Lights that are all aglow
A natural phenomenon of green, white and red
An observable fact indeed it is said

This splendid array of colours and light
That just captivates and fascinates
This force of energy that silently cries
And spans the distance of the northern skies

With draping curtains and brightness of light
An act is portrayed to a silent song
A regal display of a dance composition
I watched this show in fascination

This wondrous sight a show of force
Sometimes portrayed as a sign from God
A sight perhaps of a heavenly battle
Or a beautiful act of a laser recital

THE OLD BALLROOM

I hear a band a-playing
The sounds they are of old
I closed my eyes and listened
To the symphony music played

Then there before me this I see
A handsome stranger stands
With a bow and a smile he stretched his hand
And into his arms took me

Not a word was spoken – not even a sigh
As he danced me round – I was on a high
The graceful movements so elegantly done
The sounds of the waltz the band played on

One last turn – and then he was gone
The sounds of the music then died down
My eyes opened and I looked around
At the derelict ballroom I just danced around

The phantom dancer – the phantom band
This old dance hall – a taste of the glam
Of days gone by and charms of olde
It still tells a tale this ballroom old

THE OLD BOWLER HAT

What's that on your head? – I was asked
As mocking remarks are made
I touched my bowler and caress it softly
As tales start flooding back

Tales I was told of how it was made
The shape and the reason why
And the many heads that it protected
From obstacles in days of yore

Tales I was told of who wore them
And of how it won the West
Where lawmen and outlaws all alike
The 'Old Bowler' – on their heads

Royalty, Ministers, and Comedians
Private Detectives and all
This hat on their head with the walking cane
A feeling of dominance given

This old icon of the past
And a history that it possesses
So proud of it, to be wearing it
My precious bowler hat

THE OLD WOMAN

Early in the morning as the clock strikes four
You'll hear her sing as she starts her chores
A fire she'll make of wood and sticks
Then the bread she will start baking

Early in the morning when the clock strikes six
One chore is done and another has begun
This age of old a pail she carries
As water she'll fetch from the watering hole

While the others eat she'll rest her weary feet
Before she gets going, the start of 'clothes washing'
Her hands full of corns, her legs full of veins
Her years this life of keeping, and still she keeps on singing

THE REASON WHY

Why do you sing so sad, so sweet
Like a nightingale in the night?
Why shed tears so silently you
From those eyes so radiantly blue?

My son, he's off to war, he's gone
My boy of twenty-one
To fight for a nation not of his kind
This thought it comes to mind

With guns, and drums, and hand grenades
I saw him off with his brigade
And then you ask me why I cry
That sir is the reason why

My tears I'll shed till he comes back
My songs I'll sing so sad
For when he's back – alive, not dead
They'll never take him again

No gun he'll carry – no drum he'll beat
No grenade again he'll throw
No tears to shed – no songs to sing
For to war he'll go no more

So until then I'll be this way
While my poor boy's away
These songs I'll sing, these tears I cry
Until I see him again

THE ROSARY

You come in all shapes and sizes
Be it plastic, glass, or wood
But what is your meaning I ask myself
But to aid in prayer and reflection?

We use you in recital
We hold you in our hands
You're made up of a cross and beads
Attached to a piece of string

We hold the cross and say 'The Creed'
And then the 'Our Father'
To the Blessed Mother ten 'Hail Mary's'
We'll recite this to the end

Each decade of you whilst we pray
Is a meditation of redemption
Of He who suffered and died for us
And for those in need of compassion

This blessed rosary will always be
A call for prayer and song
A comfort region to be in
She'll never let you down

THE ROSE THAT CRIED

I smell your fragrance
A pure sweet perfume
I follow this scent
And it brought me to you

You're beautiful and charming
Then I see your thorns
This weapon of yours
Is sometimes unappealing

I look and stare
At the raindrops on your coat
Slowly they fall
Like teardrops from the heart

I watch in amazement
At the picture I see
I see a rose that is crying
For me

THE SEVEN SINS

Gluttony, Anger, Greed and Lust
Sloth, Pride, and Envy
These vices we are warned against
So why do we practice them?

The desire to consume more than we need
While others starve and malnourished
The yearning to possess wealth and power
To show and keep for oneself

The hunger for the pleasures of the body
With no concern for diseases
And then there's 'anger' not well liked
But we'll pay the price for the outrage

The wish to have what others has
And the jealousy that's expressed
Yet we idle ourselves and neglect to do
That something that needs to be addressed

And then we come to the worst of all
That's 'Pride' in all its glory
Love for oneself – disdain for the other
Why do we yield to them?

THE STILL OF THE NIGHT

In the still of the night I watched you dance
As you sing to a haunted tune
The pain in your eyes – the sorrow of your heart
The song for a love that's gone

In the still of the night I keep watching you
My only thought but to comfort you
But as I near you, you fade away
Like the mist disappearing at dawn

In the still of the night I will return
My one hope but to find you
Again to watch this silent act
In the quiet of the night you do

THE STORM

The night is dark
The atmosphere perplexing
Everything's so still
It's really quite confusing

Then out the darkness a crackling sound
That lit up the skies and all beyond
Then the booming sound of the clapping thunder
Like the devil himself riding his charger

The wind starts howling a requiem song
That seems to get stronger as it traverses along
The heavens then throw down a deluge of rain
A punishment of some kind it seems to portray

The sea then begins a frenzy dance
And seems to want to invite us all
While in turmoil it races and impacts the shore
As it rises over ridge and all in her trail

The storm's now passed and into blue skies
A picture of destruction is left to spy
The price we pay for natural disasters
When residing where was once paradise

THE OLD WORKHOUSE

Each time I hear stories of old
I tremble at the thought of the old 'workhouse'
Of all the people who enters there
And the tales of horror and despair

For the poor this public institution
Is one's worst fear of all
For once you're in – you can't get out
A fate worse than being in detention

The young, the old, the mentally impaired
The residents of the old workhouse
Where the work they did would draw blood
For a plate of food and a bed

So when you're sitting so comfortably
In the warmth of your own sweet home
Think back to the days and the 'old workhouse'
And ponder, 'Could I have done that?'

THOSE TO HEAVEN SING

Those that never doubt or fear
Those that know of death and tears
But underneath that cross they bear
Those to heaven sing

And all the pains they have endured
And as the sun sets end of day
Underneath that cross they bear
Those to heaven sing

Their time has come and this they know
And in their minds they pray
For underneath that cross they bear
The road to heaven they sing

THUNDER – THUNDER

You're violent and you're fleeting
And go with sister lightening
You're often very hostile
And dance with rain and hail

You can be beneficial
You can cause devastation
Either way – a storm
Of high definition

Thunder, Thunder, mighty thunder
Hostile you're in passing
Along with sister lightening
A dance with hail and rain

TIME WITHOUT END

What is time?
What is End?
What is time without End?

Is it a growing perception, a cessation or conclusion
Or compared to an endless realization

Where did we come from, where are we going
They say there is no beginning and that there is no end

So what is time?
What is End?
What is time without End?

TIME

Time is an observer
Time is a bystander
Time is a dimension
Time is an expression

Time is a moment
Time is an instant
Time is an occasion
Time is an illusion

TO WATCH YOUR SON DIE

As I trudged that road to Calvary
I reached out to hold your hand
And try I did but could not reach
As they pushed and shoved you away

As I trudged that road to Calvary
I watched your son as he fell
He did three times as he carried that cross
And each time they mock and jeer

As I trudged that road to Calvary
I hear you call his name
Your hands outstretched – you tried to reach
But all of this – in vain

As we reached the road to Calvary
I see you grimace in pain
Your eyes are shut but your tears streamed down
And a silent cry as the hammer hits down

I stood there on this Calvary road
And I watched as you look at your son
A painful message you sent to him
'We knew this time would come'

And as they took him from the cross
And laid him in your arms...
You took the crown of thorns from his head
And you washed his wounds with your tears

I watched as you cradled him 'neath that cross
Your tears I see – your pain I feel
And there at the end of Calvary road
Your words I hear – 'It's done – my Son'

TROUBLED MIND

Why do you sit there in the dark
With your head hanging low?
That look on your face – one of pain
And the lines, the lines they show

Who are you that sits in the dark?
Your eyes, they open wide
That constantly probe the shadowy night
What do you see, I wonder?

Your voice, your voice as you mumble to yourself
A discussion with whom, I question?
Your hands, you just keep wringing them
And a message, frantic for attention

How is it you have ended up here?
For sure you were not there
For once you were sane and now insane
And trapped in your own state of mind

TRUST & ABUSE

We trusted you, we trusted you
So why mislead you did
Our dearest friend who's always there
One we all depend on?

When you, you had your troubles
We helped each way we could
We stood by you all the way
Till your issues were resolved

Now this new found freedom of yours
Seemed but to distort your mind
For 'abuse' and 'betray' new tricks of the trade
Is the name of the game now played

People all around us,
Years of trust and dependence
But do we really know them
Too late when you find you don't

This lesson of 'TRUST', be very wary
When called upon between friends
From those that are so dear to you
An accord that can go wrong

So look after yourself, tell no one
Your thoughts you keep to yourself
For if you trust the one by you
For sure you will get hurt

UNTAINTED

I come to you untainted
For you who I love the best
I am but a new white rose
My blossoms to you I give

I come to you untainted
I kept myself so pure
I knew this day would arrive
When you would come my way

I come to you untainted
And I'll dance just for you
I am like the pure snowflakes
I'll caress your face with a kiss

I come to you untainted
I'm there just for you
I am like the mountain water
I'll wash your cares away

To you my love I give myself
I am all of these things
Innocent, virtuous, pure, and sweet
Untainted – that's my name

WEEP FOR A CHILD

A child conceived beyond a dream
A journey of expected bliss
A beautiful babe with a cry so sweet
A world she enters of wickedness

The first few years of cuddles and kisses
A mother's arms there to protect
A rock to and fro and a song so sweet
She soon falls gently in a deep safe sleep

Off to school she will then go
To learn the ways of a brand new world
But on this road she will but meet
An army of anarchist out to compete

The next ten years of this her life
A volume of schooling she'll absorb
Where 'right' beats 'wrong', for life's not a song
In this ugly world she now belongs

Her teen life she'll find is non-existent
But this she does not know…
For the meaning of a true teen queen
Is spent most of her time indoors

Her life's about to change though
As rebellion now steps in...
She's found the chance to have some fun
And escape the refuge and love within

A taste of wine and mixed cocktails
She finds quite attractive
A new self-belief is in the making
And a strong risk just worth taking

She's gone one further and found something new
A cocktail of drugs – that travel they say
It makes you forget – hurting and all
Her senses now – are all disarrayed

And now she's lost and nowhere to be found
An impending search has now begun
A mother weeps as she rocks back and forth
For a child she bore but now is gone

WERE YOU?

Where were you when he carried that cross
This cross so heavy it weighed him down?
Were you one of them that egged him on?
Were you – were you?

When he looked at you, blood gushing from his face
From the crown of thorns that was placed on his head
Did you jeer and laugh with the mocking crowed
Did you – did you?

Now he hangs there crucified, a painful executing
A death so slow, and so agonising
And when it was over they all ran in fear
Were you one of them – were you?

WHEN THE DEVIL RIDES

Heroin, LSD, Crack, and Cocaine
These are the drugs that can cause you pain
The Devil aides that makes you his
A bizarre trip of a state of bliss

This journey one takes with the devil himself
Where pain, hunger, and grief, and fear
Where the chill of the cold cannot be felt
And even the loss of self-respect

A presence is created when he's around
And right and wrong is not unknown
When the devil himself is at the helm
And takes control of all your souls

When the devil stops and asks for a ride
Be strong enough and turn him down
For if you do your soul you'll find
Is one more captured for all time

WHEN THE DOGS MEAN MORE

A gift from God the richness of all blessings
Are the children you bear from a joint union
Where love is bestowed whether right or wrong
And the father and mother are all in one

But when the new arrivals they join our home
And all the excitement is all but done
The dogs he said are man's friend best
He never mentioned the extent of 'how'

Where the kids are concerned – there's no more look in
But the dogs were always in
His attitude as if he births the dogs
And not his own true kin

The dogs on the bed and under your feet
The dogs get brushed and push you around
The dogs – the dogs – the b—y dogs
Obey none – but him

There must be a law on man's attitude
Between his dogs and his kin
They are man's friend I am but sure
But to live like this – I just abhor

WHEN THE SKYLARK SINGS

When dusk meets dawn and the gentle breeze flows
And the morning sky with its blush of many coats
The sounds can be heard so very, very, clear
Of the dawn birds singing – their songs so rare

My mind comes awake and I listen with enchantment
My eyes kept shut at the know of pure enjoyment
But one clear sound that the wind does bring
Is that special song that the skylark sings

As the thoughts fill my head her sweet sounds I hear
I will speak to her and my soul I'll bear
Not to stop singing for joy to me she brings
Each time I listen when the skylark sings

WHERE SLEEPING BONES LAY

(*The Catacomb*)

Way, way down in the underground
A city of the dead there lay
With miles and miles of snaking tunnels
And bones that once carried souls

This resting place of many a mortal
Be it child, woman, or man
Martyr, murderers, thieves, and saints
A place they all have gone

Many a story has been told
And as to the reasons why
It is but yours to believe
The learning's of the past to life

But in these tunnels you will find
A language you'll speak so silent
Where pictures of life you will see
In a place of perpetual night

A sacred place – an evil place
I know which to believe
For as I exit this soundless place
A sanctuary of peace I feel

WHILE BETHLEHEM SLEEPS

While Bethlehem sleeps so silently
A baby child was born
Out in a stable one cold night
And lay in a crib of stone

His mother and father Mary and Joseph
A watchful eye they keep
On this young child through the night
For a reason he was destined

A choir of angels they did sing
Of the birth of this new born king
Glory, glory, glory on high
A message of peace they bring

Three wise men, they had appeared
And reverence to him they paid
Laid down their gifts of gold, myrrh
And frankincense as he lay there

This special season of advent time
Our thanks we give for his birth
The joys to know he came to save us
And to know the hope of heaven

WHILE MARY SINGS

I hear a baby crying
Sweet sounds I hear this night
And the voice of an angel singing
A song so calm – so right

This song that's sung, so sweet, so low
These words of a lull-a-bye
Tu-ra-lu-ley – Tu-ra-lu-ley
Hush now and don't you cry

Close your eyes – my little one
Let sleep just kiss your eyes
So hush my babe and do not cry
As I sing you a lull-a-bye

Mary and Joseph – a vigil keep
This blessed holy night
Over the little infant there
And the star – it shone so bright

While the baby sleeps – Joseph will watch
And Mary – she just sings
Jesus is born – hail the glad morn
For Our Saviour, Christ the King

WHO'S THERE?

They live in shacks – the ground is their bed
The little one's lie – not a pillow for their heads
A fire will burn – a means to keep warm
A means to cook on – its light will protect

Hardships there lie and no comforts of life
A way of existence from a country afar
Where children are seen as beasts of burden
As water they carry for miles and miles

Who's there for these people when disease hits them by?
Who's there for these people when they lie down and die?
The look in their eyes as the flies settle down
As their feeble arms try – to swipe them by

Who's there – who's there – is anyone there
As this way of life is revealed to us all
Where people live as they call out for help?
Who's there – who's there – who's there?

WHY MARY CRIES

Mother Mary – I call on you
And ask you your opinion
This blessed night – your son was born
To save all people from sin

But then O Mother – why those tears?
Your breast heaves with sadness
Is it because your son has died
For a people whose guilt just rides?

Now on the entrance of man's domain
Lies signs of love and pain
Where drugs and guns are all the game
And his message seems all in vain

Mother Mary, Mother of God
My eyes are full and dim
Pray for us sinners now and forever
That we find the message in Him

WHY WON'T THEY LISTEN?

When my child I give advice
Please show me how to do
For when I do I cause such a rift
For that they don't want to know

I think of the past when they call
Whenever they are in need
I wipe their tears and soothe their woes
And make them well again

They're older now and all have gone
A new home they have found
I watch and see them make mistakes
Just as I did when I was young

The problem here is this you see
The error of their ways
The retaliation in their eyes
How dare I question why

They make me feel – I've stepped out of line
A message not to get involved
I am now the kid once more
The way my child has spoke

I get the feeling to leave them be
To find the error of their ways
But I'm afraid it is too late
They're constantly asking aid

Do I refuse and keep at bay
And leave them to their demise?
A parent's guilt will then be aware
An ache so hard to bear

So tell me please – I need to know
As to why they just won't listen
I should be there in their time of need
But what if they don't pay heed?

WHY?

You run around, your faces covered
The cowards that you are
You rape and plunder at any hour
The cause of all your horror

It doesn't matter, your life, you think
Is useless and of no worth
You embrace knives, bullets and guns
And you don't care who gets hurt

The pleasure and high – all this you feel
When an evil deed is done
And a mother weeps when her child's gunned down
As tears wash the blood from her fallen son

And then you have the nerve it seems
To plead mercy for the crime you've done
What thoughts were in your head, she begged
When you pulled the gun and found her son?

Who gave you the power where the wicked rule
Whilst you relish the sounds of the painful cries
Of all your victims that were wasted in the night
By your abysmal portrayal of power and might?

And as this woman buries her son
Wouldn't be surprised your presence isn't there
As you raise a bottle to the one gunned down
Whilst already preparing to load your gun…

WISH I WERE YOU

To tell me that he loves me
To know that he loves you
As we walk down the isle
Whilst he wishes I were you

A smile on his face
As happiness is portrayed
And all the time
He wishes I were you

Time has gone by
And my life's all forlorn
For his true meaning of love
Is wishing I were you

If I could make him happy
To know my love's worth
How can I compete
When he wishes I were you?

YOU OCEAN WAVE

You ocean wave – you demolish
You ocean wave – you ravage
And when you do it's so surprising
You come without a warning

You are accountable for many lives' loss
You wipe out homes and constructions
How something so calm and beautiful
Can cause so much destruction

You ocean wave you're so serene
With colours of different hues
Then out the blue you rise in wrath
And may God aid all in your path

2012

Here we are again
A new year's just begun
What's in store for me I ask?
I ponder at the thought

As I look back at 2011
And things I did not do
Resolutions made but failed to do
It always is the same

So 2012....
This year you'll find me thus
I'll choose my way and do what I can
And take action when I must

100 YEARS ON

In the year 1830
Poverty was the game
History has made it known
In the workhouse was your name

In the year 1940
A harsh war was fought
Every man, woman, and child
In service they were caught

In the year 2020
There's talk of cars flying
Will we respect or eradicate
Or name this year the new making?

www.ingramcontent.com/pod-product-compliance
Lightning Source LLC
Chambersburg PA
CBHW060253050426
42448CB00009B/1629